Harold Fulton Ralphdon

The Age of Cleveland

Harold Fulton Ralphdon

The Age of Cleveland

ISBN/EAN: 9783337427252

Printed in Europe, USA, Canada, Australia, Japan

Cover: Foto ©ninafisch / pixelio.de

More available books at **www.hansebooks.com**

THE

AGE OF CLEVELAND

COMPILED LARGELY FROM

CONTEMPORARY JOURNALS AND OTHER ORIGINAL
SOURCES

And Edited for the Benefit of Posterity

BY

HAROLD FULTON RALPHDON

NEW YORK

FREDERICK A. STOKES & BROTHER

1888

EDWARD O. JENKINS' SONS,
PRINTERS AND STEREOTYPERS,
20 North William St., New York.

TO

BIG FRED AND LITTLE FRITZ

This Book

IS DEDICATED.

PREFACE.

It is no unusual occurrence for some antiquarian, after the lapse of several centuries, to seek to construct an historical review of a past age by means of its contemporary journals, prints, novels, magazines, and other similar literature. The imperfections of such a method of historical research are manifold and various, of which the first to suggest itself is the author's inevitable lack of personal familiarity with that period which it is his purpose to chronicle. He is, therefore, though actuated by the most impartial motives, liable to exaggerate the importance of trifles and underestimate the value of more important

events accordingly as they are magnified
or minimized by the literature of the period.

Moreover, the authorities which such an
historian finds at hand are not always of the
highest order.   In spite of that optimistic
view of the survival of the fittest it is un-
fortunately true that society is occasionally
very indifferent to its contemporary literature and ofttimes injudicious in its preserva-
tion, not infrequently permitting that to be
lost which would be of incalculable value
to the historian of the future.   It is scarcely
possible to overestimate the loss which the
literature of Greek social, political, and literary life suffered in the destruction of the
plays of Agathon. Many perplexing phases
of the influence of the sophists in politics
would be capable of explanation, the final
development of dramatic art more easily
traced, and additional light thrown on several obscure passages in the comedies of

Aristophanes, had the age of Pericles been less indifferent to the productions of its great contemporary, the earliest representative of the fictional school of tragedy.

Although the art of printing has, by multiplying the number of copies of a book, materially lessened the chances of its destruction, the root of the evil remains unchanged. Every age disregards the lessons furnished by the past and exhibits equal negligence in failing to select and preserve such of its current literature as will convey to posterity a vivid and accurate impression of its varied and multiform life.

There is, moreover, another circumstance peculiarly calculated to be a fruitful source of error to whoever undertakes in the future to write a history of the present age. Contemporary journalism must necessarily supply the principal materials for such a history, and it is scarcely reasonable to expect

posterity to be familiar with the various oc-
cult methods of advertising which are such
a prominent feature of that class of literature. Yet ignorance in this direction must
lead to mistakes not only laughable, but
positively injurious to the reputation of my
own times. I have often, for example, re-
flected upon what disagreeable consequences would ensue if posterity should
be unacquainted with the present use of
the reading notice. The future student of
our history might naturally conclude from
the prominence given to the discussion of
the merits of different proprietary articles,
and the editorial comments on the same,
that the present age is far more interested
in soap than religion, and in perfumery
than in politics.

Again, journalism presents the news of
the day in a compact and abbreviated form,
furnishing a mere outline which the intelli-

gent reader can accurately fill in from his personal familiarity with all the details of current events. Such an outline is admirably suited for present needs, but is marred by the serious fault, that it is apt to convey a totally wrong opinion to those readers who have no acquaintance with such details. A parallel case is to be found in those sketches of distinguished citizens which adorn the columns of many of our most popular dailies. To the personal friends of the subject of the sketch they convey the impression of a very accurate likeness, whereas a total stranger would be in doubt whether they were intended as a portrait of a district attorney or of the greatest showman on earth, and might fall into the pardonable error of imagining that a citizen of Bridgeport had been elected to the head of the criminal department of the city of New York.

For these considerations I have deemed
it advisable to write a history of my own
times. One purpose in so doing, is to supply what may be termed the *res gestæ* of
contemporaneous events. I have, in other
words, endeavored to impartially record
those circumstances which are regarded as
trite or trivial, by contemporary journalism,
and accordingly omitted entirely.

The book is therefore in no sense designed for my contemporaries, who will no
doubt find it a tedious chronicle of events
so familiar as to be wholly without interest;
but exclusively for posterity, whom I am
sanguine enough to expect to be grateful
for these exact memorials of an age which
seems tame enough to us, but which will
no doubt be magnified into great importance through the telescopic vision of time.

I have not deemed it necessary to enu-
merate the various cyclopedias, biographies,

handbooks, and other volumes of statistics, not to mention pamphlets, reports, almanacs, and similar paper-covered literature which I have consulted in the preparation of the present work. It is sufficient to say that I have drawn largely for my information upon our great dailies and current periodicals, so that it may be truthfully said to be brought down to date.

I have, however, deemed it of importance to explain a rule of syntax which has been adopted. As I have compiled this volume for the exclusive benefit of posterity, the secondary tenses are obviously appropriate in chronicling events for such a constituency. As it is my intention, however, to publish my book at once, it seemed equally imperative to employ the primary tenses. The necessity for choosing between these two alternatives caused me no little anxiety, for no one stands in greater

awe of the critical spirit of the age than do
I. Even such insignificant circumstances
as blunders in punctuation, and typograph-
ical errors, are apt to lead to serious consequences. The omission of a comma has
been known to nullify a statute, and the
unauthorized insertion by a printer of a
vowel-point in a Hebrew noun is sufficient
to jeopardize a whole system of theology.
Grammatical errors are likely to so mo-
nopolize the attention of the critic that he
can devote but scant space to the review
of the book itself. If the present age is
so critical, it is appalling to think what it
will be in the future. My perplexity was
naturally great, for I desired to avoid having my book irretrievably condemned for
what would be at the best but a mere fault
of style, and could in nowise affect the
matter. After no little consideration, I
concluded to uniformly employ the primary

tenses. Such a rule of syntax is eminently
suited to my contemporaries, while it cannot fail to lend an air of realism to the volume when it comes to be perused by posterity. I trust this frank explanation will
serve to disarm the hostility of any critic
who may be inclined to question the propriety of my syntax on the ground that the
primary tenses have been employed to describe events which must necessarily belong to the past, when my book obtains
that constituency for which it is specifically
designed.

I would simply add, in conclusion, that
I have at all times tried to assume a neutral position on the questions which I have
attempted to discuss, and although it has
been necessary in a few instances to dis-
close my personal convictions on some
particular subject, I have earnestly endeavored to make no statement which I

myself have not, as far as it was possible, carefully verified, and have conscientiously avoided creating a false impression, not only by a positive violation of the truth, but by guarding against that tendency to exaggeration which is such a serious fault in the historian.

HAROLD FULTON RALPHDON.

GROONKAY, N. Y., *February*, 1888.

CONTENTS.

THE GENERAL CONDITION OF POLITICS.

THE GENERAL CONDITION OF POLITICS.

BEFORE entering into any detailed discussion of the principles and condition of the political parties of the present age, I have deemed it prudent to anticipate and correct certain errors into which posterity might possibly fall from a perusal of our contemporary literature.

For this reason I desire to state at the outset that Grover Cleveland was President of the United States during the period covered by this chapter. I make the statement with considerable reluctance, for I am of the opinion that posterity, upon reading it, will be inclined to seriously question my reliability as a historiographer of my own times. For it requires no effort

of the imagination to foresee the indignant
and emphatic protest which this statement
will elicit a century hence from every pure
and simple-minded patriot who is familiar
to any extent, either by personal examination or by tradition, with many of our contemporary journals. "What!" such a
one will exclaim; "this incarnation of
guilt and incapacity, this corrupt politician,
who never said a wise thing, and always
did a foolish one, the successor of the
blameless Washington and the martyred
Lincoln! It is preposterous! The partisanship of the American people could never
have so mastered their patriotism as to
have permitted his election. There is assuredly some mistake."

Yet, incredible as it is, I am compelled
to reaffirm the statement that Grover
Cleveland is, to the best of my information
and belief, President of the United States

in the year of our Independence the one hundred and twelfth.   I cannot make the statement absolute, because I was not present either at the official canvass of the votes of the various electoral colleges by the joint Houses of Congress, or at the ceremony of inauguration.   But I have seen certain acts, messages, and public documents which purported to be signed by him in the capacity of Chief Magistrate. I have also heard him frequently alluded to as President, and occasionally spoken of with respect.

I have likewise deemed it advisable to make the statement that Grover Cleveland did not bear arms against the government of the United States in the years 1861–65. It is not within the province of the impartial historian, whose function is simply to record external events, to enter into any analysis of the finer motives of human conduct, and determine whether Grover Cleveland's loyalty during these years was actuated by prudence or patriotism. But, as a considerable portion of the current press has been negligent in observing the metaphysical distinction between act and intention—a species of negligence which cannot mislead those who are familiar with all the facts—I have considered it prudent to thus enlighten posterity, lest future generations might confound moral culpability with overt guilt, and imagine that Grover Cleveland and Jefferson Davis were one and the same person.

It is also appropriate to state in this connection that Grover Cleveland was not connected with any of the Ku Klux raids in the South during the period of reconstruction. To this affirmation I am able to bring the irresistible support of very strong circumstantial evidence. A cursory examination of a map of the United States, supplemented by a careful study of the facilities of transit between Buffalo and Louisiana during the time of the existence of that marauding organization, will prove that the time consumed in travelling between these two points would have been so great as to make it an impossibility for a citizen of Buffalo to have been present at any one of these raids without rendering himself conspicuous by his protracted absence from home. I am therefore convinced that in this instance Grover Cleveland can successfully prove an *alibi*, and I may add that in this opinion, a considerable number of my contemporaries who have impartially examined the facts in the case, heartily concur.

It may, however, relieve in a measure the mortification of posterity to learn that Grover Cleveland was, after all, only *de facto*

President of the United States, and that ample evidence of the worth and incomparable superiority of our *de jure* President during this same period will be found in not a few of our daily and weekly journals. For the benefit of posterity I will explain these two terms. A *de facto* President is one who receives a majority of electoral votes. A *de jure* President is one who would have received such a majority, had not the will of the people been defeated by the action of a Returning Board, an untimely speech of a clerical constituent, or some other untoward or unforeseen circumstance wholly incommensurate with the dignity of a presidential election. The duties connected with the two offices are also dissimilar. Those of a *de facto* President are to conduct legislation in the present; those of a *de jure* one to shape politics in the future.

For fear the point might be raised here-
after, I have deemed it advisable to state
in this connection that up to the present
month (February, 1888), no question has
been raised as to whether our *de jure*
President did not work a forfeiture of his
office by visiting England and France during the present year.   Such an extra-terri-
torial residence would seem to be contrary
to the letter, at least, of the law forbidding
the President to depart from without the
jurisdiction of the United States during his
official term.   I am not a lawyer myself,
and cannot therefore determine the question from a strictly legal point of view.   I
would, however, suggest that, had any
sufficient grounds existed, the many enemies
of our *de jure* President would have been
quick to insist upon his removal from office, and that their failure to do so furnishes
strong presumptive evidence of the ab-

sence of all such grounds.   Moreover, the
example of Mr. Tilden can perhaps be
pleaded as a precedent, for he made a protracted visit to Europe after his inauguration in the preceding March.

I am sincerely solicitous for the sake of
the honor of my country, that posterity
may find in this suggestion of the distinction between *de jure* and *de facto* an effi-
cient means of escaping from the awkward
and humiliating predicament of acknowl-
edging Grover Cleveland as the twenty-
second President of the United States.   I
am not sure but that it has occurred to
many of my fellow-countrymen equally
patriotic with myself, but I believe I am
the earliest to elevate it to the dignity of a
principle.   It is surely infinitely better
founded than a thousand and one other
legal distinctions, and certainly no more
difficult to be comprehended by a layman

than many of the decisions of the highest
courts of record in the various States of
the Union.

I am also anxious to anticipate and correct another error into which posterity
may possibly fall. There was no civil
war in the United States in the year 1887.
I have deemed it advisable to make
this statement, because I opine that the
future historian of our country, when he
comes to that passage in our history which
is known as the Veto of the Pension Bill,
and the Order to return the Rebel Flags,
and reads the fierce denunciatory curses
which made historic Harlem ring, the bel-
ligerent resolutions of G. A. R. Posts, and
the angry threats of old war Governors,
will impatiently turn the subsequent files
of these same journals in order to learn the
details of that bloody and fratricidal strife
which he confidently expects was the log-

ical consequence of such an universal out-
burst of indignant patriotism. It is to relieve the perplexity of such an one that I
make the definite, unqualified assertion in
this place, that there was no civil war in
the United States in the year 1887, although this is of course intended as no in-
timation that the circumstances did not
furnish an adequate *casus belli*. I must,
moreover, confess that I have never had
it satisfactorily explained to me how a
repetition of the terrible years of 1861–65
was averted. In the absence of any other
explanation, I would venture to suggest
the following, which, although candidly
admitted to be of my own personal invention, must be understood as founded upon
a careful consideration of all the facts
in the case. The McGlynn matter, the
Queen's Jubilee, the opening representa-
tion of the Fall of Babylon, all providen-

tially occurred at this juncture, and happily served to relieve the overcharged feelings of the nation as a lightning-rod attracts to itself the bolt which threatens destruction to the house, and dissipates its deadly fluid into the ground.

Having thus disposed of certain errors concerning contemporary politics, into which posterity might naturally fall had the foregoing explanations been omitted, I will proceed to a brief review of the principles of the political parties of the present age.

The two great parties are the Republican and Democratic,* although there is a third, commonly called Mugwump.   This

---

* In using the words Democratic and Republican, I must be understood as referring only to the Simons Pure of each party.   I have not deemed it necessary to record the views of those Moderates who are being constantly ground to pieces between the upper and the nether mill-stones of the Extremists.

last party has no machine, and is consequently expected to have no principles.   It
is therefore extremely difficult to define its
exact position in municipal and national politics.   A Mugwump may perhaps, however,
be defined as a Gallican in politics, who
is constantly irritating the Ultramontanes
of his party by voting *non placet* at Republican Primaries.   It is in fact the party of
dissent, and regards with a curious lack of
reverence many of the most cherished tra-
ditions of both parties, notably those which
relate to the importance of the machine and
the intimate and intricate connection between good government and a partisan
civil service.

The vital distinction between the Republican and Democratic parties is that the
former insists that the war is not yet over,
the latter that it has never taken place.   I
cannot emphasize too strongly the necessity

for posterity familiarizing itself with this distinction.   If it is ignored the substantial foundation for much of the virulence of the current press of the period can never be appreciated.   For it would otherwise seem both absurd and illogical that two parties who are so perfectly agreed that the Chinese must go, that seventy-two cents make a dollar, that the laboring man is entitled to fifty-two half holidays during the year, and that eight hours' work deserves a ten-hours' wage, besides exhibiting equal unanimity on various other questions, should nevertheless be so bitter toward one another that a member of one party is never mentioned in the official organs of the other, except in terms of unmeasured contempt, and his memory when dead, accorded less respect than is usually given to that of a valuable setter or favorite race-horse.   But such mutual hostility is perfectly intelligible to us, as it will be to posterity, if that vital distinction between the two parties which has been noted above, is only kept constantly in view.

One of the most distinctive principles of the Republican party is that of protection. Not only does it insist that home manufactures need to be protected against the pauper labor of Europe, but advocates with equal vehemence and persistency, that the negro requires protection against his former master; a disunited North protection against a solid South; the people of the United States protection against a Democratic President; the President protection against his own party; the people of the State of New York protection against a Democratic Governor; the liquor-dealer protection against the Prohibitionist, and the Prohibitionist protection against the Personal Liberty League. I am quite con-

vinced, from such examination as I have
been able to make, that no other party,
either past or present, was ever more be-
neficently paternal in its purpose and its
scope.

Another principle equally Republican in
its character, although of more recent origin,
is that of political entail, or that a man is
entitled to a nomination because he is the
son of his father.   The genesis of this doc-
trine is not to be traced, as has been imputed in certain hostile quarters, to a confession of paucity of candidates possessing
sufficient merit of their own to entitle them
to the honor of a nomination, but to that
great principle of the party that the war is
not yet over.   The most ordinary conser-
vatism would naturally influence any party
to select in such a critical state of affairs,
only those candidates whose loyalty is as-
sured beyond all question, not only by pred-

ilections of a personal nature, but by that great principle of heredity which science has demonstrated to be the controlling force in human conduct.

Yet, however great may be the difference between the two parties on certain domestic issues, they are nevertheless in complete accord in regard to what should constitute an appropriate foreign policy. Both unqualifiedly approve of Home Rule for Ireland. Perhaps of the two the particular plank in the Republican platform which touches on this subject is a trifle more unequivocal, for it mentions Gladstone and Parnell *eis nominibus*, whereas they are not specified at all by name in the corresponding plank of the Democratic platform. This is naturally a matter of just pride to every Republican, and simple justice requires it to be said that it is perhaps due to the direct or indirect influence

of our *de jure* President over this party,
who, though he has been charged at times
by his enemies with indifference to events
at home, is conceded by both friend and
foe to be unequalled at flying the American eagle in foreign affairs.

In order to explain the *raison d'être* of
what follows in this chapter, it becomes
necessary to violate that principle of strict
neutrality which I have conscientiously
striven to uniformly observe elsewhere
throughout this volume. By reason of my
party affiliations, I am bound to believe
that another term of Democratic rule, with
its systematic indifference to the importance of G. A. R. Posts, and unseemly des-
ecration of Decoration Day by fishing
excursions, can only terminate in the over-
throw of all constitutional government, the
successful establishment of the Confeder-
acy, and the restoration of slavery. Re-

cent events have caused me to view with unfeigned alarm the constantly increasing chances of the election of a Democrat to the Presidency in 1888. It is in view of such a catastrophe that I have been influenced to write the remainder of this chapter, thinking that posterity might feel a melancholy interest in the examination of the Constitution of our one and indivisible Republic before it had been split up into innumerable petty States. I have not, however, deemed it necessary to literally transcribe the various provisions of our Constitution, or furnish a detailed description of our present form of government. I will not admit, even to myself, that the sectional hate of the Solid South, who, though former slaveholders, are still Americans, will ever attain such depth of intensity and malignity, so that when the sad day of its supremacy arrives, it will endeavor to systematically obliterate all memorials of the past. It is scarcely probable that the various volumes containing copies of our Constitution will, immediately after the final success of the rebel arms, be burned by the common hangman in the city of Richmond, and any allusion to the past forbidden under severe penalties, as a toast to the exiled Stuarts, in the days of the Commonwealth, sent a loyal cavalier with short shrift to the headsman's block. I have deemed it reasonably certain that copies of our Constitution, surviving the dismemberment of our Union, will be easily accessible for the inspection of posterity, and that a general recollection of our present form of government will be transmitted from loyal sire to loyal son. But I desire to call the attention of posterity to that unwritten constitution, that higher law, of which no exact memorials

exist, and the memory of which even tradition cannot be expected to preserve when
State Sovereignty has become supreme,
and Federalism a mere dream of the past.

First of all, I wish to refute a slander
which has obtained a wide circulation in
our day, and may possibly find an echo in
the sounding corridors of time. It is a
standing reproach among European nations
that the United States is wholly indifferent
to the class of foreigners which she wel-
comes to her shores, and makes no distinction between what would and would
not form a desirable addition to her population. The origin of such a serious mis-
statement may be readily traced to that
ignorance, prevalent in all monarchical
countries, of the high value placed by us
on our Elective Franchise, which rests
not upon intelligence or thrift, but upon
simple citizenship. It is therefore only

logical that the immigration of all who possess capacity for citizenship, even though
it be in an imperfect and embryonic state,
should be welcomed as a substantial addition to our population, while the presence
of those who lack this important qualification should be distinctly discouraged.   That
this is no fanciful distinction of my own,
invented to excuse what has been frequently urged as a reproach upon my
mother country, is fortunately capable of
easy demonstration.   For how else is it
possible to explain the policy of extermin-
ation adopted toward the Indians, or the
stringent laws forbidding the immigration
of the Chinese?   It is therefore appropriate to state at this point that both the In-
dian and the Chinese are regarded as ex-
cepted from all the benefits conferred by
that clause of the Constitution which pro-
vides that no State shall "deprive any

person of life, liberty, or property without due process of law, nor deny to any person within its jurisdiction the equal protection of the law." I am especially anxious that posterity should note this exception, as it affords the only possible explanation of the paradox that a people so sensitive to constitutional rights as to resent the indignities of prison clothing, discipline, and fare to which Mr. O'Brien was subjected at Tullamore Jail, should view with apathetic unconcern the outrages on life, limb, and property, to which two classes of their own population are not infrequently subjected.

The intimate connection existing between the Declaration of Independence and the Constitution of the United States may perhaps justify a brief allusion to a limitation recently attached to one of the clauses of the former. It has been judicially decided that the pursuit of happiness, specifically stated in the Declaration to be one of the inalienable rights wherewith all men are endowed by their Creator, does not extend to the happiness of getting drunk on Sunday or to that of killing policemen with dynamite.   I have regarded it as not superfluous to make this statement, as a perusal of certain current petitions, open letters, and legislative memorials,—a class of literature which seems to possess great tenacity of life,—might, in the absence of all knowledge of the real facts in the case, create a directly contrary impression. I have for this reason deemed it prudent to record in this place that it has been judicially decided in more than one instance that the happiness of getting drunk on Sunday is not such an inalienable right but that it can be abridged by local legislation, and that so high a tribunal as the Supreme Court of the United States has held

that fanatic principles justify homicide not
one whit more than a quick temper or any
other equally unromantic cause.

As has been hinted above, it is especially
difficult for the writer of contemporary
history to observe that strict neutrality
which is rigidly required of the reliable
historian. The extent of that difficulty
may be perhaps appreciated by reflecting
that many historians of periods which are
separated by several centuries from that
of the author, have, nevertheless, been
unable to view such distant events except through the colored medium of their
personal sympathies and convictions. The
names of Mr. Mitford and Mr. Grote will
readily occur as examples of this very serious fault of introducing into historical
composition what is in effect a species of
anachronism.   Yet if the historian, detect-

ing an analogy between the political parties of ancient Athens and those of modern England, can be influenced by his Whig or Tory sympathies in his estimate of statesmen and philosophers of an age as remote as that of Pericles, it is not, surely, surprising if the writer of contemporary history should at times depart from the narrow line of a strict neutrality in the discussion of events in regard to which he has at some prior time assumed, in all likelihood, a positive and personal position. But even such a temptation is less subtle in its character than is still another which assails the historian of his own times. He is a part of the age which he depicts, and consequently feels a certain amount of personal pride in it. The temptation is therefore strong to soften, if not wholly conceal, such flagitious acts and circumstances as would seriously reflect upon the reputation of that age.

I have ventured the foregoing prelude to the concluding part of the present chapter, for the purpose of explaining the disagreeable position in which I am now placed. For it has become necessary to record at this point a state of affairs which will justify posterity in believing that our beloved Republic, with her much vaunted equality of all citizens in the sight of the law, is at the best but a pretentious sham. It has almost seemed to me as if my duties as an historian scarcely required me to record so shameful a fact. I have been able to find but slight consolation for the sense of injury done to the reputation of my age and country by my scrupulous regard for the truth, in the reflection that an exhibition of veracity in a direction so manifestly disagreeable must serve to convince posterity that this history, be its other faults as thick as dust, is at least reliable.

I would therefore reluctantly state that an opinion, involving in a peculiar degree the reputation of our Republic and stigmatized in 1864 as treasonable and disloyal, has in the year 1887 not only obtained a wide-spread circulation, but the refusal to accept it is viewed with suspicion as indicative of absolute disloyalty. I refer to the opinion that the war is a failure. In order that posterity may appreciate the weighty consequences involved in such an opinion, it is wise to be explicit.

It had long since been admitted that the war is a failure from any stand-point of preserving the Union. The reconciliation which was effected between the North and the South at Appomattox, has for many years been viewed as purely formal, as a mere outward show of peace and good-will, under which sectional hate bubbles and burns as fiercely as ever. Although

forced from this point of view to admit
that the war is a failure, it was customary
for every pure-hearted patriot to find a
certain amount of comfort and gratulation
in the thought that the war is a confessed
success, in that it secures by the Fifteenth
Amendment the right of suffrage to the
negro.   But it is now no longer possible
to conceal the fact that the war is a failure,
even from this stand-point.   Humiliating
as it is, the truth inexorably requires the
confession to be made that the right of
suffrage is not simply occasionally or local-
ly denied the negro in the South, but systematically and universally.   I am aware
that such an accusation involves a serious attack upon the integrity, honor, and
loyalty of a large portion of our population.
It in fact implies the commission of such
heinous crimes that I feel as if I had a right
to ask posterity to demand no further proof

of its truth than my uncorroborated statement. For no one, unless actuated by
motives of unparalleled malevolence, would
venture to make such an accusation except
upon evidence so convincing as to make
any other conviction impossible. The accusation has, in fact, obtained considerable
circulation in our day by the weight attached to the personal word of the accus-
ers. I frankly admit that within the past
year I have never seen produced in its
support a particle of evidence of that formal and solemn character which is required
to convict a citizen of the violation of a cor-
poration ordinance. The wide circulation
which this accusation has obtained, is due
in a large measure to the unsworn statements of men whose social and political
position is so high, whose professions of
regard for the reputation of our Republic
are so profuse, and whose protestations of

interest in our national prosperity are so
fervent, that incredulity would be almost
a reflection upon their personal honesty
and integrity. I have, however, decided
to depart from the example set by these
gentlemen who largely constitute my authority for bringing this accusation, and
produce evidence of its truth.* Before
doing so, I must, however, first caution
posterity to avoid certain natural errors of
judgment, which would make a proper ap-
preciation of the value of this evidence
impossible. Posterity must disregard the
sworn statements of many Southern citizens
of excellent repute, must reject as worthless
the official reports of several Congressional
committees, and above all, attach no value

---

* I must distinctly disclaim all credit of being the
original discoverer of this evidence. I have heard it
used on more than one occasion, although I am unable
to state to whom the credit of its original discovery
should be given.

as a precedent to the decision of the Electoral Commission, whereby it was decided that the properly certified returns of any State were such conclusive evidence of the regularity of an election as not only to exclude any legal action in the shape of a *quo warranto*, but as having such moral weight as to forever elevate the question from the region of debate. If the example of the present age in this direction is followed, the weight of the evidence which I am about to produce will be as apparent a century hence as it is now.

This evidence is based upon two principles, that of population and that of heredity. Before entering into any specific explanation of the former, I have deemed it wise to make another cautionary statement. The zeal of some few of my contemporaries has not infrequently betrayed them into a certain intemperance of statement, wherefrom it might be inferred, that if there were a fair count in the Southern States, every one of those States might be relied upon as invariably giving a Republican majority. That is scarcely an accurate view of the case. By the principle of population the character of the present majorities of the two States of South Carolina and Mississippi, would alone undergo a radical change. This is in a measure irrelevant, but I have ventured to make the statement, hoping that my frankness in conceding that even under a fair count many of the Southern States would still be entitled to a Democratic majority, may serve to convince posterity that my conviction of the absolute nullification of the Fifteenth Amendment south of Mason and Dixon's line, rises to the dignity of a principle, and is not simply the result of a bitter and intemperate partisanship.

The principle of population may be briefly stated to be a comparison of the black and white voting population of any State, with the certified returns of that State. The method of arriving at practical results may be succinctly stated as follows. The negro, if unintimidated, will always vote the Republican ticket. This proposition rests largely upon the principle of heredity to be shortly explained. Hence, by comparing the total Republican vote in any State with the total number of colored electors in that State, it is an easy matter to exactly determine to what extent the negro has been denied the right of suffrage by either actual or constructive intimidation. It is from such a comparison, made by myself personally, and based upon the official census and certified returns, that I have been forced to accept the conviction that the provisions of the Fifteenth

Amendment are systematically violated in many of the Southern States. I have not deemed it necessary, however, to furnish any tables of statistics in support of this statement. If posterity desires such confirmatory proof it will be easily found in the same original sources which I have consulted.

I shall now dismiss this branch of the subject and proceed to give a brief explanation of the principle of heredity. This principle is based upon the scientific theorem, that political tendencies are like any other physical or psychical habit transmitted from one generation to another. The importance of this principle of heredity cannot be depreciated by the easy sneer that it is purely theoretical, for it affords the only possible solution of an otherwise very perplexing political problem—*i. e.*, how many generations of colored voters must arise in the Southern States before the inherited fealty of that class to the Republican party shall entirely disappear.

The number of consecutive generations to which any peculiarity of a common ancestor will be transmitted, depends almost exclusively upon the degree of intensity which marks the presence of that peculiarity in such an ancestor. The craving for tobacco has been known to descend to the great-great-great-grandchildren of an inveterate smoker, while it is no unusual occurrence to find the immediate issue of the son of a moderate wine-drinker, uncompromising teetotalers. It is therefore necessary in the present instance to simply ascertain how strong was the loyalty of the first race of colored citizens to the Republican party, in order to determine to how many consecutive generations that loyalty will be transmitted. In order to fully appreciate this principle

of heredity, however, one more circumstance must be noted.   It is a well-known
physiological fact, that a habit which is
contracted in childhood, is marked by
much greater tenacity than if contracted
in middle age or even in early manhood.
The value of this fact is evident, when it is
remembered that the negro contracted the
habit of voting the Republican ticket during the very earliest stages of his political
infancy.   The strength of that habit will
become equally apparent from the most
superficial acquaintance with the thorough-
ness of the training whereby he was led to
contract it.

In this view of the case it is highly important for posterity to become familiar with
that vigorous and systematic instruction
furnished the negro at the very outset of his
political life, that it was his solemn duty to
invariably vote the Republican ticket, and

that his failure to do so, on the occasion
of even such an insignificant event as a
local election, was not only a species of
ingratitude without parallel and a tacit admission of his readiness to return to a
state of servitude, but an act of unequivocal encouragement to his former masters
to revive the *ancien régime* with all its hor-
rible accompaniments.   It is surely reasonable to believe that a habit contracted
through the powerful agency of such painstaking and thorough discipline, should be
transmitted to one succeeding generation
at least; it is not difficult to conceive of its
transmission to several consecutive generations, so that until miscegenation, climate,
or other physical causes shall have inter-
rupted or neutralized the operation of this
law of heredity by completely changing his
status, the negro, unless intimidated by actual violence or unlawful threats, will never

of his own free, unaided choice vote the
Democratic ticket.

Although I have studiously avoided
burdening posterity with cumbersome and
uninteresting tables of statistics or the citation of special cases, I cannot refrain from
calling attention to an occurrence of recent
date which I regard as of considerable
value in refuting the many stringent and
hostile criticisms continually passed upon
the intelligence of the negro as an elector.
Many Northern voters of more than average intelligence seem to be unable to comprehend the exact position of the Republican party on the question of the saloon in
politics. That excellent *via media* of prohibition without prohibition, is not infrequently lost sight of. The blunder of
many of my contemporaries in imagining
that prohibition pure and simple, without
any negative limitation, is a distinctively Re-

publican principle, led to consequences of a serious character in the fall elections of the past year. Yet the negro of the South exhibited far superior intelligence in that direction. For when that issue was raised in Atlanta at a recent election, he voted steadily against prohibition, presumably on the ground that it was obnoxious to his Republican principles, as he of all others was the most benefited by the absence of saloons in that city.

THE STATE OF SCIENCE.

THE STATE OF SCIENCE.

I AM sufficient of an egotist to believe that I have had the good fortune to be born in what is destined to be regarded as the Saturnian age of Science. Moreover, the modern spirit of scientific investigation is marked by a catholicity of effort no less surprising than brilliancy of achievement. Science has, in fact, taken the entire range of human comfort and convenience for her especial field. A famous anatomist had no sooner proclaimed the triumphant discovery of a method for locating abscesses on the brain, than a distinguished specialist announced the invention of a system of clothing manufactured upon strict scientific and sanitary principles, and calculated to materially aid in the physical

regeneration of mankind. Subjects as varying in quality and degree as the virtues
of cocaine as an anæsthetic, whereby
operations should be rendered painless,
and shoes sewed on anatomical lasts,
whereby locomotion should be made easy,
each and all receive the same earnest, re-
spectful attention of contemporary science.

The simple enumeration of the mere
titles of the various inventions of this
prolific age would require entirely too
much space, while anything like an accurate or intelligible description of them all
is wholly out of the question. Nor have I
deemed it necessary to furnish even such
a catalogue of titles. There is a full and
accurate index of patents in the office of
the Commissioner at Washington, and the
systematic date kept of the record of the
filing of the caveats, makes it extremely
unlikely that the present age will be de-

frauded of the credit for any invention which has been properly patented.

But there is reasonable ground for apprehension lest in the case of those discoveries which are unpatentable in themselves, and of those for which the inventor, either through negligence or poverty, failed to secure a patent, a certain amount of confusion may arise, and the reputation of the present age suffer a positive injury by posterity arrogating to itself the credit for discoveries which undoubtedly belong to contemporary science. Nor shall I attempt to describe all such discoveries, many of which, I frankly admit, may never have come under my notice, but shall confine myself to a description of those alone which are not ephemeral in their nature, but destined to retain their novelty a century or so.

The dual discovery that there is no God

and no personal immortality, may be said to be the chief of the many brilliant achievements of science, although, perhaps, the honor of the first must be shared with an earlier age. For, if certain ancient chronicles are to be believed, the credit for this discovery must be given to an anonymous individual who lived some three or four thousand years ago, and although he was generally regarded by his contemporaries as a fool for entertaining such an opinion, he must, in the light of the most recent researches in biology, be considered as having been several centuries in advance of his age. I have not deemed it necessary to enter into any discussion of the credibility of these ancient chronicles with a view to determining in what period of history this discovery was originally made. I shall content myself with simply calling the attention of posterity to one incontestable fact. Even if a past age must be credited with actually originating this discovery, that cannot detract in the least from the glory which belongs to my own. For contemporary science has been the first to make this discovery of any practical utility by popularizing it, so to speak, thereby bringing within the reach of all what had heretofore been monopolized by a few progressive minds.

I have sometimes wondered whether posterity will be so prodigiously grateful to us, after all, for these two discoveries, as we are wont to imagine. Belief in Providence used to be a mighty comfort, and the obsolete view of regarding the life of the present as simply the beginning of an eternal sentient existence seemed to furnish about the only satisfactory solution of very many vexatious problems. Experience, moreover, appears to teach that mankind are not so completely controlled by a disinterested desire for knowledge as to feel grateful for the explosion of a pleasant fiction by the discovery of a disagreeable truth. I have ventured these remarks for the purpose of explaining any traces of resentment which may occasionally exhibit themselves in this chapter. I frankly admit that I once believed myself to be an immortal soul, and I must confess that this discovery of the contrary aroused in me such violent feelings of mingled rage and disappointment as to make ignorance seem infinitely preferable to wisdom. I shall, however, make an honest effort to lay aside my personal feelings and discuss this whole subject with the strictest impartiality of which I am capable.

Another discovery of great importance, is that of an original and exact definition of life. By reason of the long-standing misapprehension that human and animal life were wholly different in their origin and scope, the former had been made the subject of many flattering beliefs, and come to be regarded as something akin to divinity. But science, by a persistent and exhaustive examination of crustacea, oysters, and apes, has finally succeeded in distinguishing between the true and the false by accurately defining life as a connexus of organic activities. Although this definition is a trifle mortifying, in that it obliterates all distinction between man and the mollusk, it has, nevertheless, had a clarifying influence, serving to dispel many illusions of long standing, and working a complete revolution in all prior notions of ethical laws. Drunkenness, murder, and theft are now no longer viewed with that childish and superstitious horror with which such phenomena had inspired former generations, but simply as imperfect manifestations of these organic activities, which, under a totally different environment, would have been developed into temperance, philanthropy, and honesty; just as flesh, brilliant in coloring and exquisite in texture, differs not one whit in organic structure from that which, through imperfect development of the tissues, degenerates into cancer.

It seems to me scarcely possible to overrate the importance of this discovery, that mind and spirit are simply finer forms of matter.   I am, in fact, quite convinced that it is destined to exercise a wide influence over the conduct of men in the future.   It is, therefore, only natural that I should desire to emphasize that the credit for making it may be justly claimed by the present age.   It is for this reason that I desire to call the attention of posterity to

a recent work by Herr Tüdelsdorf, entitled
"Das Verhältnisz Zwischen Moral und
Magen," or, in the translation, "The Connection between Morals and Stomach."
This valuable contribution to the literature
of exact science is at present known to
only a select few, although I am much surprised at its limited circulation, for it pos-
sesses all the essentials of an extensive
popularity, since the author is a foreigner
by birth, and is both realistic in his descriptions and heterodox in his sentiments.
The purpose of the book is to prove that
morals are a mere matter of diet. The
author, a distinguished biologist, and at
one time a professor in a German univer-
sity, but for many years a resident of the
United States, spent considerable time in
perfecting his theory, and has recently
made public the results of a long series of
experiments, which are alike interesting

and convincing. The subject of these experiments were, with but few exceptions,
notorious housebreakers, murderers, anar-
chists, and similar outcasts of society. It
follows, therefore, that the book should
contain the latest information concerning
the habits, thoughts, modes of life, and
peculiar *argot* of the criminal classes ; and
as the distinguished author is not troubled
with any modish scruples of propriety, the
style is the very perfection of art in its
naturalism. As has been hinted above, I
cannot understand why the volume has not
attained a wide circulation, but I wish to
assure posterity that not only are its contents well known to all advanced thinkers
of the present age, but that the conclusions
reached by the distinguished author are
fully and unreservedly accepted by such.
There is space here for only the most
meagre summary of the contents of this

volume, which I am confident is destined to supersede the " Pilgrim's Progress " and "Paradise Lost," on the book-shelves of the next generation. This summary is not, of course, furnished for the instruction of posterity, but is inserted in this place simply as proof that contemporary society is familiar with Herr Tüdelsdorf's great discovery, and that the credit for it properly belongs to the present age.

A falling apple first suggested the law of gravitation to the inquiring mind of Newton ; and the discovery of many of the principles of science has been due to circumstances equally trivial. The case of Herr Tüdelsdorf is no exception to that rule. A law-abiding citizen, and conservative in his politics, he was on one occasion, when walking through the Thiergarten at Berlin, seized with a sudden and unaccountable mania for assassinating the Kaiser. The suggestion horrified him in the extreme, but, try as he would, he was unable to expel it from his mind, and even went so far as to walk in the direction of the Schloss. By a prodigious mental effort he finally succeeded in so far regaining control of himself as to retrace his steps, and at length reached home in a state of nervous excitement bordering on delirium, and trembling with the apprehension that his brain was softening. As he entered the house he was suddenly seized with severe pains in the stomach, accompanied with nausea, and he mixed himself a glass of pepsin and soda, which brought him immediate relief. With the cessation of his physical pains the regicidal mania, which had given him such alarm, also vanished. He then made an effort to recollect if he had eaten anything unusual during the day, and suddenly remembered that he had partaken heartily at dinner of some bologna sausage highly seasoned with garlic,—a dish which he subsequently learned, by the merest accident, was a great favorite with the German socialists. The synchronism between the disordered condition of his stomach and anarchical frenzy led him to suspect that the connection between the two was causal and not accidental. He accordingly determined to test the matter still further, and partook on the following day of bologna, dressed in an exactly similar fashion. The result was in a measure startling. There was a recurrence of the same disagreeable physical symptoms, and violent regicidal mania, and relief from each was only obtained by recourse to pepsin and soda. A still further incident served to convince Herr Tüdelsdorf that he was on the verge of one of the greatest discoveries of the age.

He noticed that his youngest daughter, Gretchen, a mere child, in the nursery, of an unusually amiable disposition, and careful in an extraordinary degree of her playthings, was, when suffering from the colic, not only subject to violent outbursts of temper, but greatly given to destroying everything which came within her reach. Subsequent investigation in this direction, as well as his own personal experience, ultimately served to convince the Professor that all kinds of anarchical sentiments were due entirely to the colic in some form or other. An exhaustive monograph which he published, containing an account of his investigations up to this point, attracted considerable attention, and he finally secured permission from the Director of Police to make an actual application of his theory upon the prisoners confined on the charge of socialism in the prison at *Plötzen See.* The result was satisfactory in the highest degree. The method pursued was curative, and not diagnostic; for the Professor had determined to reduce his theory to practice by a practical demonstration, that all forms of anarchical frenzy could be permanently cured by the same remedies employed for the relief of colic. The four subjects whom he had selected for purposes of experiment were the reddest and most radical communists in Europe, yet in less than a year they were converted into law-abiding citizens of a highly conservative type by small doses of soothing-syrup judiciously and methodically administered under the personal direction of Herr Tüdelsdorf.

The Professor then enlarged the scope of his investigations so as to include the entire field of ethics. Shortly after his removal to the United States, and at about the same time that a distinguished contemporary had announced that all nervous diseases were due to the imperfect focusing of the eyes, he completed and published his *magnum opus*, which proves, by a multitude of experiments, that all immoralities are entirely due to a disturbance of the normal proportion of acid and alkali in the stomach.

I must now hurriedly pass over the various other discoveries made by science in the present age. I would, however, beg posterity not to construe the limited space assigned to their description as any reflection upon their relative importance, but to regard it as due entirely to the brevity necessarily imposed upon me by the size of the present volume.

By the fact that it was capable of a certain amount of verification from the past, the discovery of Natural Selection has attracted considerable attention. For this discovery placed in an entirely original light a custom which had prevailed to a considerable extent in former years. I refer to *mariages de convenance.* As man is an animal, his sole object in mating must be that the deficiencies of one of the parties should be supplemented by the acquirements of the other. In view of this fact, it is easy to understand how *mariages de convenance* are in exact accord with the highest scientific principles. For thereby the poverty of one of the contracting parties is relieved by the wealth of the other; the *bourgeois* blood of the husband neutralized by the aristocratic descent of the wife. It is, however, a little curious that the custom should have fallen into disrepute at about the same time that the only scientific explanation of its existence was discovered. There can be no question,

however, but that this present abeyance is
only temporary, and that *mariages de convenance* will be resumed in the future,
when they will attain a still greater pre-
cision, inasmuch as they will then be wise-
ly regulated by scientific principles and not
by mere rude instinct as in the past.

But the greatest and most original discovery of all, is that of Evolution. This
must not, however, be confounded with
Natural Selection. Both were, it is true,
invented by the same man, but, although
apparently identical, they are in reality
related to each other as is cause to effect.
The limited space which I would be per-
force compelled to assign to any description of this great discovery, might be
misleading. The conspicuous absence of
any details might, in fact, justify the inference that my estimate of the magnitude of
this great discovery is greatly exaggerated.

I will therefore content myself with making a single cautionary suggestion and refer posterity for all further information on this subject to those large octavo volumes wherein the subject is exhaustively discussed, and also to the recently published life of the inventor. For I am confident that the voluminous literature of the subject will outlast my own generation for a considerable time and be easily accessible for inspection a century or so hence.

I would therefore caution posterity to avoid the error, which is not uncommon in our day, of imagining that the descent of man is the only phenomenon capable of explanation by evolution. It is infinitely more ambitious in its aim and scope, seeking to furnish a sufficient reason for every phenomenon, small or great, in the universe. All progress in Belles Lettres and Philosophy is clearly shown to be but the result of evolution. Moreover, whenever the productions or talents of an individual author interfere with the horoscope cast by the evolutionists for some particular age, science does not dogmatically seek to prove his existence a myth or endeavor to depreciate his abilities into that dead level of mediocrity required by the laws of evolution, but charitably accounts for his appearance by the clever supposition that he was a hybrid. States, with their complex constitutions and societies, with their delicate and elaborate machinery for the protection of life and property, have been proven to be the evolutionary result of bardic meetings in the past and the blood-money of the original German tribes; while in the philosophy of cooking, the origin of the miracles of pastry art constructed by our modern *chefs*, has been definitely retraced through successive and gradual stages of development to the mud-pies of the primitive Aryan race.

Having ventured to exhibit a certain amount of personal irritation at the commencement of this chapter, I should be guilty of an unpardonable injustice, did I omit to specify the unquestioned benefits which accrued from many of the discoveries made by science. Although all belief in a conscious immortality had long since been destroyed, science nevertheless holds out the hope that according to the Conservation and Correlation of Energies no life, however insignificant, is wholly lived in vain. Man and the mollusk, it is graciously hinted, contribute alike indifferently toward keeping the world in a condition of active motion, which would otherwise fall into a very perilous state of sloth. I

am sadly conscious of my inability to bring
to the discussion of this biological conception of the universe anything like that degree of enthusiasm to which the subject is
entitled. I can only plead for my lack of
ardor that the discovery is of comparative-
ly recent origin, and that the memory of my
discarded belief in a future state plagues
me with an uncomfortable sense of the in-
adequacy of a posthumous and impersonal
contribution to the kinetic energy of matter, as a substitute for personal immortality.
But *tempora mutantur, et nos mutamur.*
Habit is a facile magician, and the next
generation will no doubt entertain feelings
of a very different character on this subject. For when the leaven of this new
gospel has had time to work, men will
view death with exceeding peace and
calmness, cheered by the thought that the
bones, which St. Paul and eighteen sub-

sequent centuries fondly hoped would be clothed upon with immortality, will not vainly perish, but by being converted into excellent fertilizers, materially improve the digestion of coming races, and that the cunning chemic cells, once supposed to be the habitation of an immortal soul, will furnish a superior kind of phosphate for the relief of overtaxed brain-workers in the future.

It is, however, pleasant to be able to record that although science destroyed the world's hope of immortality, she has greatly facilitated the means for the attainment of a painless longevity. Never in the history of the world as at the present time have such numberless laboratories been in active operation for the manufacture of pain-killers, extracts, syrups, plasters, and other infallible cures for all organic diseases. The marvellous rapidity with which such articles are manufactured is only excelled by the low price at which they are exposed for sale, and thereby brought within the reach of both rich and poor. In fact, in even the present age the cost of prolonging life easily and painlessly to a considerable term beyond the traditional threescore years and ten, is much less than that of Christian burial formerly, and it is only reasonable to expect that greater opportunities still, will be offered in this direction in the future.

Moreover, the opinion that increased facilities for the attainment of longevity might prove a comfortable substitute for immortality, seems to have found in even our day a certain amount of confirmation in quarters least expected. For I have noticed that many religious newspapers have begun to devote their columns, heretofore exclusively reserved for the discussion of themes of a spiritual nature, to advertisements of sarsaparillas for the blood, pads for the liver, and protectors for the chest.

THE MORAL, INDUSTRIAL, AND SOCIAL CONDITION OF THE AGE.

THE MORAL, INDUSTRIAL, AND SOCIAL CONDITION OF THE AGE.

A DISAGREEABLE and humiliating task awaits me at the very threshold of the present chapter. Any picture of the condition of contemporary morality, must, if faithfully limned, be absolutely repulsive to such as have the slightest respect for even conventional decorum. The foulest excesses are an every-day occurrence. Murder, bigamy, theft, and similar crimes are on the constant increase. The instincts of our population are of the lowest order. Our moral degeneracy is, in fact, so complete that the most sanguine has lost all hope that temperance, honesty, and virtue should ever become our national traits once more.

I feel confident that I have exhibited elsewhere in this volume sufficient indications of patriotism and personal pride in my age, to convince posterity that nothing except an irresistible regard for the truth would induce me to bring such charges of turpitude against my contemporaries. It is only by evidence so conclusive as to admit of no denial that I have been forced to accept such shameful conclusions.

That evidence has been furnished me by a great metropolitan journal, the sworn circulation of which is simply stupendous. I have been forced to construe its popularity as convincing proof of its reliability. Any other course would have convicted my countrymen of being either fools or knaves,—that is, as either so credulous as to be unable to distinguish between true and false news, or as so lacking in all reverence for the truth as to lend their support to the publication of protracted falsehoods and misrepresentations. Apart from my unwillingness to place such an unflattering construction upon the character of my contemporaries, the continued success of that journal soon convinced me that either of these two propositions was untenable. A fraud is always short-lived, and time alone is required to make a liar tiresome even to those who are themselves wholly indifferent to the truth. The constantly increasing circulation of that journal was, therefore, accepted by me as an additional proof of its reliability.

I must admit that it has required no inconsiderable effort to overcome my natural reluctance to expose the unwholesome condition of contemporary morality. My feelings on this subject have in fact been so strong that I have resorted to various expedients whereby I might be enabled to

truthfully modify my views. I, for instance, made a systematic search to discover some ground for believing that the
policy of this journal was purely sensa-
tional, and that it therefore only sought to
record those events which became tragic,
because of their criminality, or startling,
by reason of their sensuality. But I
speedily became convinced that I had no
reasonable ground for such an hypothesis.
I was forced to conclude, from the profuse
and passionate claims to impartiality put
forth by this journal—to the sincerity of
which so many of my contemporaries had
attested by their subscriptions—that it was
wholly without likes and dislikes, that virtue and vice were viewed by it from the
same impartial stand-point of news, and
that, if the record of good and fair actions
found only an occasional place in its columns, this was entirely due to their rarity

in real life, and not to any editorial aversion to their publication.

It is no occasional or spasmodic examination of the columns of this journal which has led me to form such a damning opinion concerning the present state of morals. That opinion has been formed only after a careful and systematic daily perusal for a period of more than two years. It is too much to say that I have been unable to discover a single action which dignifies human conduct recorded during that time in the columns of that journal. But those which I did find were of such rare occurrence, and the space allotted to them was so brief, that they would have wholly escaped my attention had I not been on the constant alert to discover some instance of virtue and decorum, however insignificant, to relieve the blackness of the long catalogue of crime.

I would that I could relieve myself of all personal responsibility in this matter, by disclosing the name of my authority, which, for prudential reasons, I have deemed it best to withhold altogether. To be frank, I am afraid lest posterity, becoming familiar with the various artifices employed as advertising mediums in the present age, would view this volume with a certain amount of distrust, did I specify that journal by name. It might, in fact, suggest the suspicion that this history, which I have conscientiously endeavored to raise to the dignified level of an impartial record of events, is no history at all, but simply a novel species of editorial enterprise on the part of that journal, invented for the purpose of increasing its circulation by publicly advertising the large space reserved in its columns for the discussion of scandals and crimes. It is in view of some such insinuation being made that I have deemed it pertinent to distinctly affirm, in this place, that neither this chapter nor this book is written in the interest of any daily or weekly journal. I will make that affirmation stronger by the additional statement that I have no affiliations—social, political, or literary—with any member of the newspaper press.

I have also considered it wise to explain at this point why it is that, in discussing the subject under present consideration, I have contented myself with general allegations, which, though, I trust, are sufficiently unequivocal to be explicit, are conspicuous for an absence of all details. Another reason than a feeling of repugnance toward lingering over a subject so manifestly painful, has influenced me in this respect. Although it was possible to comment on many vices and crimes with perfect frankness and unlimited freedom, I would still have had to confine myself to the widest generalities in the discussion of one class of immoralities. It is only simple justice to state that this would not have been due to any lack of particulars in the journal constituting my authority. That class of immoralities are described therein with painstaking attention and patient regard for the most insignificant items. Caution alone has prompted me to take this course, for I was quite unable to determine, with any degree of certainty, to what extent the Society for the Suppression of Vice would permit me to indulge in details. Nor need posterity be at all surprised that what can be printed with impunity in a journal claiming to have half a million of readers, cannot be safely published in a book which can never hope to attain such an extensive circulation. The paradox will become at once intelligible if a single important distinction is only noted. It is agreed in the present age that the most extravagant license of theme and treatment is not only excusable, but commendable, when used for the dissemination of news; whereas the same license, if employed in a formal contribution to literature, is promptly rebuked as injurious to the public morals. For this reason, I deemed it prudent to avoid any possible risk of collision with that Society which might result in causing my book to be suppressed within ten days after publication. That Society, therefore, and not I, must be held responsible for the vague treatment which this whole subject has received at my hands, as it seemed ridiculous to exhaustively discuss some topics, when, by the very nature of things, I would be compelled to dismiss others of equal importance with the most general

allegations. Having made this explanation, I shall now turn from this very disagreeable theme to the discussion of another infinitely more pleasing to me.

It would be unnatural for any one having
the prosperity of our country at heart, to
curb in the least his fervent expressions of
thankfulness for our recent safe deliverance
from a most serious industrial crisis. I
am not, of course, unaware that such an
intrusion of personal feelings is, from a
strict point of view, slightly unprofessional,
and apt to be regarded as inconsistent with
that judicial attitude which the historian is
expected to uniformly observe. I am confident, however, that posterity will view with
a kindly eye any effusion of enthusiastic
pride, which it were well-nigh unpatriotic to
suppress, in describing our narrow escape
from a predicament of such a critical nature

as to threaten for a time the stability of our government. As a familiarity with the gravity of the situation is necessary in order to appreciate the sufficiency of my grounds for congratulation, it is pardonable to minutely describe the condition of affairs which culminated in such a serious crisis.

It had been surmised for a long time by the more astute observers of current events that there was on foot a secret but well-developed plot to betray the United States into the hands of Great Britain. "Trifles, light as air," if viewed as detached circumstances, but of weighty moment if regarded as parts of a coherent whole, had not failed to attract considerable attention in certain quarters. The unpatriotic indifference exhibited in the Fisheries Dispute, the negligence in providing proper and adequate coast defences, the erection of a monument to Major André on American soil, and the

unconcealed admiration of Mr. Lowell for
British society—these, and many other in-
cidents which might be easily cited, were
highly suspicious as evidences of some oc-
cult scheme of disgraceful treachery ; just
as the indications of gneiss at occasional
intervals on the surface is sufficient to convince the geologist that an excavation of
the soil will reveal a continuous stratum of
that primary rock.

Although subsequent events fully justified such prognostications, only a few were
sufficiently far-sighted to discern from the
first the omens of coming danger. The
people at large, lulled into a false security
by the deceitful indications of coming prosperity, pursued their wonted avocations,
oblivious of the sword of Damocles suspended above their heads. But on De-
cember 6, 1887, the slight thread by which
that sword was suspended was rudely sev-

ered, and it fell with an ominous clatter, bringing consternation and panic to the American people. On that day, to drop all metaphor, our *de facto* President made public the contents of his annual Message to Congress. I would remark here that I have no desire to impugn the motives of our *de facto* President, for I feel as if he were entitled to a certain amount of respect by virtue of his position. For this reason I shall not dwell, as have many of my contemporaries, upon the latent suggestions, hidden meaning, and general tenor of that Message, from which the inference would be clearly deducible that the author must have been influenced to write it by the promise of a large subsidy from the English government. I shall therefore content myself with the statement of undisputed facts, leaving the analysis of motives to some other historian.

The unequivocal encouragement given by that Message to British industries was patent on its face. Not less patent was the evidence which it furnished of a foul conspiracy for the final destruction of the Union. Moreover, the audacious details of that conspiracy, as revealed in the Message itself, were a surprise even to those who had had their suspicions already aroused. It was now apparent to the most sceptical that the ultimate purpose of the Anglo-American Cabal was to completely beggar the country by free trade, when by reason of its exhausted condition it would fall an easy prey to the gun-boats of the British navy.

The blackness of that day will scarcely admit of exaggeration, recalling, as it did, the deep despondency which prevailed at the North at the time of the attack on Fort Sumter. It is not indeed too much

to say that the gloom was even more intense. The prospect of our glorious
Union, rent with civil feuds, and drenched
with fraternal blood, was hard enough to
face. It was an infinitely more bitter
thought that our Republic, born from the
throes of revolution and fostered into a
great commercial commonwealth by a system of wise and generous protection, was
destined to degenerate into a mere terri-
torial adjunct of Great Britain. What
disgrace could be keener than that thirty-
eight States should be treacherously de-
prived of that independence which had
been won a century before by only thirteen,
at the cost of unparalleled heroism and
self-sacrifice ?

Such gloomy thoughts were to be read
on every countenance. The mechanic cast
his tools on his bench, the weaver left his
loom, the shoemaker dropped his last,

each and all disheartened by the thought
that the time was not now far distant when
the laboring man in America would be
compelled to work for pauper wages and
die in a pauper workhouse. The actual
injury done to great industrial enterprises
was of a serious nature. I shall, however,
leave it to the statistician to formally record
how many factories shut off steam, and
how many furnaces banked their fires in
consequence of this Message. An atmosphere of absolute panic prevailed. Men
sorely felt the need of help, but where was
help to come from when the *de facto* Presi
dent of the United States had shown him
self to be an open sympathizer with the
Anglo-American Cabal?

But help did come. "The land laughs
with applause," to quote the felicitous
phrase coined by one of my contemporaries in describing the present crisis.

The revulsion from tears to laughter, from gloom to glee, was quick, but none the less genuine and sincere. Moreover, help came from the only source whence it could be expected to come, although it involved an economic paradox. A dual executive is usually considered a menace to constitutional government. In the present instance it proved our salvation. For shortly after the formal transmission to Congress of the annual Message of our *de facto* President, the annual message of our *de jure* President was transmitted to the American people. The latter outlined a policy directly contrary to that which had been indicated in the former. Its effect was electrical. Men of varying and diverse conditions,—the poorest laborer, the more prosperous shopkeeper, the wealthy manufacturer,—lost all fear. Confidence succeeded panic, for the prophecy

made at the time of the nomination of our
de jure President had been literally ful-
filled.   Nothing more was needed than
the presence at the helm of such a "calm,
deliberate, commanding, sagacious man,"
to give the fullest assurance that the old
Ship of State which seemed destined but
a few days before "to go down beneath
the waves forever, carrying her precious
freight with her," would now surely "come
into her harbor, into still water, into safety."

I have purposely refrained from tran-
scribing in full this message of our *de jure*
President.   In the first place, I am not quite
sure that it has received the author's latest
revisions ; and I am, moreover, confident
that it is destined to be reverently cherished
by succeeding generations, as the Mag-
na Charta which saved the liberties of the
people in 1887, and will therefore be easily
accessible for the inspection of posterity.

There is one feature of it, however, to which I desire to call particular attention. Posterity must not regard this message as the unofficial utterances of a simple American citizen. Such a view of the case would furnish sufficient grounds for believing that I had either exaggerated the gravity of the situation or magnified the importance of the message itself. For it would naturally seem incredible that the personal opinions of a single individual could have so powerfully swayed the destinies of fifty millions of people. It is, therefore, with no intention of disparaging the broad statesmanship apparent in every page of that message that I emphasize the fact that it was the official position of the author as the *de jure* President of the United States, which lent it such a potent influence. Moreover, the subsequent revelation that the policy of our *de jure*

President met with the approval of one member of his cabinet at least, contributed in no small degree toward fully restoring public confidence. For, on January 4, 1888, our *de jure* Secretary of the Treasury, in his annual report to the Senate of the United States, expressed his full concurrence in the recommendations previously suggested by his official superior.

. No apologies are, I am sure, required for the foregoing circumstantial account of this critical period in our history. It, moreover, serves as an excellent introduction to the discussion of our present industrial condition, to which I shall forthwith devote myself.

No one is better aware than am I of the popular prejudice which exists against tables of statistics. I have for this reason decided to depart altogether from that

formal statistical method uniformly observed by all writers on the industrial condition of a country. Such a resolution
necessarily involves the exclusion of all
comments upon the balance of trade, the
condition of agriculture, the growth of
manufacturing and mining interests, and
other kindred subjects which cannot be intelligently discussed without the aid of
tables and diagrams. I shall, for this
reason, confine myself strictly to the consideration of the condition of labor in the
present age, which, though but a single
phase of this great subject, is entirely
worthy of the exclusive attention which I
shall bestow on it.

Every one, unless lacking in all humane
instincts, must view with unfeigned indig-
nation the disgraceful anachronism presented by the present position of the

American laborer. While England, through
the persistent efforts of the late Lord
Shaftesbury, was passing law after law for
the benefit of those employed in factories
and mines, and even barbaric Russia was
relieving the hardships of her peasantry by
giving them a communal interest in the
soil, the United States can point to only
one triumphant act of legislation in the
direct interest of labor, and that is the
half-holiday law.

Posterity must not construe this conspicuous absence of all labor legislation as
evidence that there is need of none. It is
not too much to say, that at no time in the
past was the condition of the laboring
man accompanied with more peculiar hardships than it is in the present. The majority of able-bodied workmen are wholly
unable to obtain work, and such few as are
so fortunate as to find employment receive

only starvation wages. The poverty and distress which marks the lot of the laborer is pitiable. He never has a fire in winter, and his clothing is so scant and thin as to scarcely meet the requirements of decency, and is painfully insufficient as a protection against the most mildly inclement weather.

These statements are no hasty or irresponsible utterances of my own. They are made upon the authority of a gentleman who has devoted much time to the investigation of the subject, and is the proclaimed champion of labor. I am, moreover, obliged to confess that these statements, though appalling in themselves, seem cold and meagre when taken out from the rhetorical setting of pathos, passion, and invective in which they are enshrined in the various published volumes and printed addresses of that gentleman, and which I should have been gratified to

have quoted in full had it not been for two
considerations. Anything like liberal or
literal quotation would, in the first place,
have occupied entirely too much space ;
and in the second place, have involved an
infringement of the copyright monopolized
by that gentleman, the purchase of which
required an outlay of capital quite beyond
my means.

This picture of the condition of contemporary labor, though presented only in
miniature, is necessarily so black that I
cannot resist the temptation to relieve it
in a measure by recording in this place
certain instances of material prosperity
among the poor, which have by accident
come to my notice. I am confident that
in so doing I shall win the gratitude of
every intelligent and sympathetic reader.
For I myself vividly remember what pleas-
ure it was in *ante bellum* days to turn

from the sickening recitals of the cruelties practiced in cotton-fields and rice-swamps to pleasant tales of slave-life on Kentucky plantations. It is, moreover, superfluous to state that the citation of these isolated cases is not made with any intention of lessening confidence in the veracity of that gentleman whose statements I have in substance quoted. I could scarcely be expected to impeach the credibility of my own witness, even for the laudable purpose of flattering my age and pleasing posterity.

I therefore desire to say, subject to the foregoing qualification, that to my certain knowledge six car-drivers in the city of New York possess heavy winter overcoats, and as many pile-drivers extra thick flannels, and that in the discharge of certain business duties I discovered, to my great gratification, that a dozen day-laborers receive sufficiently high wages to keep their families supplied with fuel during the winter months. I am also ready to affirm that I have repeatedly read in a daily journal an advertisement offering work to such compositors as might apply at the office of the subscriber. I do not, however, place implicit confidence in the good faith of this advertisement, as it appeared in October of the past year, and may have been only a clever electioneering dodge, invented by the capitalists to impress the public with a totally erroneous view concerning the traditional difficulties of the workman obtaining work.

As has been stated above, these fruits of personal observation are in no wise intended to destroy confidence in the Champion of United Labor. It has, however, been a pleasant task to record these evidences of occasional prosperity among a class whose condition must be viewed by

posterity as infinitely more severe than
that of the villein of the Middle Ages,
and as accompanied with considerably
greater hardships than that of the serf in
Russia before the period of his emancipa-
tion.

Before dismissing this subject altogether,
I desire to correct a totally wrong impression which posterity may possibly receive
from a perusal of much of our Anti-Pov-
erty, United Labor, Central Labor, Social-
istic and Anarchical literature. The conspicuous absence of any allusion to female
wage-workers in these journals might lead
to the inference that in the present age no
woman is required to earn her own living,
or if so, that her services are so generous-
ly paid that she has no cause for com-
plaint. I am naturally loth to dissipate
any such flattering reputation for chivalry,
but the truth inexorably requires me to

admit that there is a large class of noto-
riously underpaid female wage-workers.
The only possible explanation of the paradox that five minutes' infraction of schedule
time leads to a general tie-up, while the
long hours and starvation wages of a
seamstress provoke no comment, lies in
the intimate connection between politics
and philanthropy. The absolute worth-
lessness of woman as a political factor is
regarded as cancelling all her natural claims
on ordinary humanity. I am not wholly
without hope, however, that this defect, if
defect it be, will be remedied in the future
by the recognition of the indirect relation
which women hold to politics as the possible mothers of Walking Delegates.

I have occupied so much space in discussing the moral and industrial condition
of the age, that I can only briefly sketch

our social customs and usages. Fortunately, the last-named subject will suffer no
great injury if dismissed with scant notice.
The proverb, though musty, is true, that
nothing is so monotonous as fashion and
sin, and that any effort to be original in
either must necessarily prove a failure.
The superficial forms of society are, indeed, by no means permanent. I myself
can remember many changes introduced
during my own generation concerning
questions of precedence, the proper attitude
to be observed in saluting a lady, and the
correct cut for a dress-suit. I have, however, regarded such customs as of scarcely sufficient dignity to come within the
scope of the present history. But that
dread of *ennui*, hatred of solitude, and in-
defatigable craving for amusement, which
seeks relief indifferently in Browning Clubs,
Palmistry entertainments, and Opera par-

ties, can scarcely be claimed as original by
the present age.   I have, in fact, diligently
searched for some expression of originality
in our various social customs and usages,
and failing to find any, shall dismiss this
subject altogether, after making one or two
cautionary suggestions for the benefit of
posterity.

I therefore desire to state at this point
that what is technically known as our best
society has succeeded in forming the acquaintance of not a few genuine members
of the British aristocracy.   I have deemed
it prudent to make this statement, lest
posterity might form a directly contrary
opinion from reading the frequent accounts
in contemporary journals of the ease with
which needy adventurers successfully mas-
querade as legitimate descendants of the
Plantagenets before our American population.   Such numerous instances of credulity

might, in fact, lead to the unflattering inference that our people had never had an opportunity to distinguish between the true and
the false in this particular by the presence
of a real member of the English peerage in
their midst.   This is not so.   I am ready
to make affidavit that H. R. H. Albert Edward, Prince of Wales, Field Marshal, K.
G., K. T., K. P., G. C. B., G. C. S. I., G.
C. M. G., once visited us, for I myself saw
him in an open barouche on Broadway, in
the city of New York.   Moreover, many
elder sons of families tracing their pedigree
to William the Conqueror, have made
themselves so conspicuous by their vices
or dullness, that the rumor of their presence on American soil has reached even
the seclusion in which I dwell.

Although our society is severely democratic in its structure, I would not have
posterity imagine that we are so rude as to

be wholly without any system of caste.   I
feel that there is no need to call attention
to that untitled nobility among us, which
trace their descent in a direct or collateral
line to some signer of the Declaration of Independence, or immigrant in the Mayflower.
Such genealogical claims to social pre-emi-
nence are sufficiently cosmopolitan to be
easily understood.   There is, however, one
class distinction among us which, were it
not specially noted by me, posterity might
scarcely suspect existed in an age pre-emi-
nently commercial, and a society peculiarly
plutocratic.   From a social point of view,
there is a well-recognized difference between selling goods at wholesale and re-
tail.   The vendor in the former case is
a merchant; in the latter a shopman.
Although I can truthfully attest that this
distinction is rigidly observed in excluding
and receiving applicants for admission into

society, I am forced to admit that there is considerable confusion in certain instances as to how much business makes the merchant, and how little the shopman. I am, for example, quite unable to specify, with any degree of exactness, how many hogs a man is required to slaughter, in the course of a year, in order to be removed from the vulgar plane of the butcher to the dignified level of a pork-packer.

I shall venture to close this chapter with a statement which I greatly fear will provoke the derisive laughter of posterity. There are not only several colleges and universities in our country, but a goodly number of our population are extremely ambitious to have their sons educated at these institutions of learning. This will naturally seem incomprehensible to posterity, in view of the constant fire of ridicule to which all forms of higher education are

exposed in our current press. As an inexhaustible source of wit, that subject bids
fair, in fact, to rival the old standard one
of the frailty and fickleness of woman.
A comic paper is very poorly officered
unless possessing an editor capable of ex-
temporizing innumerable witty paragraphs
at the expense of the college-bred youth,
while no minstrel troupe is too ignorant to
invent a gibe or jest at classical learning.
It might reasonably be expected that this
species of lunacy would long since have
been laughed away. Yet it is incontesta-
bly true, that not only the number of colleges in the country, but their rates of at-
tendance, are on the constant increase. I
solemnly assure posterity that no joke is
lurking in this last statement, and that it is
made, not in the spirit of the *farceur*, but
in the character of the grave historian. I
am, moreover, wholly unable to suggest

any explanation of such a paradoxical state of affairs. For it is universally conceded that a collegiate education entirely unfits a man for the duties of life, and that he has to painfully unlearn whatever he has acquired during his scholastic career. Nor is classical learning regarded as only interfering with the prospects of those destined for trade or commerce. It is also viewed as exerting a positively injurious influence over those entering what have been dignified as the learned professions. A critical familiarity with New-Testament Greek makes a clergyman dull and doctrinal, thereby putting an end to the most cherished hopes of his friends that he would become a great popular preacher. A physician knowing more Latin than is sufficient to make his prescription intelligible to the apothecary, may win the equivocal reputation of a student, but must never expect

to be a successful practitioner, while a rising young lawyer could easily cultivate the
acquaintance of all the politicians in his
ward, in half the time required for the
mastery of the Institutes of Justinian.
Why parents have persisted, and still per-
sist, in placing such a serious obstacle to
success at the very outset of the career of
their sons, I frankly admit I am unable to
explain.

LITERATURE AND LAW.

LITERATURE AND LAW.

I AM sensible that the classification of literature with law seems awkward and arbitrary, yet the heterogeneity existing between the two is, after all, only superficial. As there are certain tints which harmonize equally well with brilliant or quiet colors, so literature is of such a neutral character as to be suited to all professions and pursuits.

This peculiarity of literature is due to the fact that no special abilities or training are regarded as necessary for its successful cultivation. It would be difficult indeed to find an individual so diffident as to hesitate to pass an *extempore* judgment upon the rhythm of poetry, the subtleties of satire, the passion of oratory, and the technique of tragedy, and who would not resent, as an imputation upon his natural intelligence, the suggestion that any special education might be required to intelligently criticise such subjects. In this respect literature stands at a great disadvantage with base-ball, lawn-tennis, and roller skating. The latter pursuits have all risen to the dignity of professions, whereas the former is viewed as occupying the level of an amateur recreation, which any and everybody may cultivate with equal ease and success.

Again, literature is unique in that it has no special precincts wherein it is strictly lodged. Chemistry cannot flourish away from the fumes of a laboratory, and law withers outside the atmosphere of a court-room. But literature, like death, has all times, seasons, and places for its own. It is discussed in the halls of classic seminaries of learning, co-operates with flirting in agreeably beguiling the tedious intervals between the dances of a ball, and figures prominently at afternoon teas. The superficial and the profound, the wise and the ignorant, the dull and the brilliant, approach literature without a single trace of that diffidence so conspicuous in the discussion of those subjects which are considered of such dignity as to require the exclusive attention of the specialist.

It must be apparent, in view of the above, that the classification of literature with law is not so arbitrary as might appear at first blush. It might, I am willing to admit, have been classified with any other topic just as well. Had I had a chapter on cooking or agriculture, there would have been no impropriety in including it in that. The present classification has, however, been adopted because of the opportunity for alliteration which it affords. Nor is such a ground for classification so purely fanciful as to be unworthy of serious consideration. It is, at least, every whit as rational as many of the laws of association which prevail in the present age. No two things, for instance, could seem to be more completely divorced than hosiery and literature. Yet a goodly number of our population have discovered such an intimate connection between the two that they would go through life without a library, unless they could purchase their books at the same counter with stockings and cravats.

Having thus justified the scheme of classification adopted in the present chapter, I shall proceed to discuss each of the two subjects in their respective order.

Not only from the large circulation

which his books have attained, but upon
the authority of a distinguished critic, am
I able to assert that Tolstoi is the greatest
living author, and that the second place
must be given to M. Zola.   It is naturally
a mortification to be compelled to make
such a confession, but it will serve as a
convenient *Deus ex machinâ* to introduce
an explanation and thereby remove what
might otherwise be regarded as a reproach
to my age, by showing that such an unflattering state of affairs is due to no lack
of ability on the part of my contemporaries,
but entirely to adverse circumstances.   The
persistent opposition to realism on the part
of the Society for the Suppression of
Vice must be held responsible for our
inferiority in this direction.   Under the
present censorship of the press our American authors are restricted to such vague
and general descriptions of immorality as

would have severely shocked the Puritans, but which seem squeamish and prudish to those who have any acquaintance at all with Continental literature. I am obliged to confess that this Society impartially applies the same rules to the publications of both home and foreign authors; but then the latter have the benefit of what may be termed the principle of expurgation. I would, in view of this fact, request posterity to make a liberal allowance for our inferiority to French and Russian novelists, as that principle seriously affects all literary composition. For it is obvious that the restraint imposed by the observance of Puritan prejudices cannot but interfere with the cultivation of a fluent style. The corollary from such a proposition is equally self-evident. Although the works of foreign authors are subjected to a process of expurgation for the purpose of adapting them to the American market, their inimitable traits of freedom and ease cannot be destroyed, and that artificial restraint which is such a conspicuous fault of our home authors is wholly absent. The difference is the same as that which results from pruning off the luxuriant branches of a full-grown tree, and forcing a shrub to grow according to a prescribed model, as was actually done with many of the plants in the gardens of Versailles. In the former case there is grace and naturalism in spite of the missing limbs ; in the latter only rigidity and a painful formality.

Candor, however, requires it to be said, that the authors themselves are in a measure responsible for this inferior condition of the American novel. They are too jocund and blithe in their temperament. Their works are spoiled, beyond all remedy, by too much faith and optimism for an age which has such an intense craving for pessimism as to be satisfied with nothing short of absolute despair. Nor can I pretend to assign the cause for this blight of optimism wherewith American novelists are plagued. It may be due to too much morality, or again to too little dyspepsia. But of one thing I am certain. An optimistic novel is regarded like stage-coaches, kerosene lamps, and spinning-wheels, as belonging, beyond all hope of revival, to a past age.

Again, American poets, with one possible exception, labor under the serious disadvantage of having only a constituency, and not a cult. The difference between the two is very marked. The purpose of a cult is to clear up obscurities in an author's text, and consequently the delight of the cult is in exact proportion to the obscurity of the author. A constituency has no such object in view, but reads for either instruction or amusement, and is apt to be very intolerant of an author whose meaning is not perfectly apparent at a glance. I am quite convinced that this disadvantageous position of our American poets is not entirely due to their inability to be dull and obscure, but that quite another reason must be assigned for it. No one can know better than the American author how futile it would be under our present inquisitive system of journalism to cultivate obscurity of style and thought for the purpose of obtaining a cult. Nothing under the sun, with the exception of the proceedings of the United States Senate in executive session, can be long hid from the reporters. Editorial enterprise would be sure to discover or invent a satisfactory explanation of the most abstruse poem before the cult could gather sufficient material to justify its existence.

Although I entertain strong hopes that the present deplorable state of affairs may be speedily remedied, I nevertheless desire to earnestly impress upon posterity that the sole way in which the competition between American and foreign authors can be placed on an impartial footing, is not, as many of my contemporaries imagine, by the passage of an international copyright law, but by a revision of the Penal Code in the interest of realism, and the assiduous cultivation by the authors themselves of pessimism and a cult.

It is pleasant to be able to turn from this account of the general state of American literature, which candor has required to be disparaging in a measure, and record that, in that special department of scholarship technically known as the Higher Criticism, an American author has recently surpassed all foreign competitors.   German scholars

had heretofore, by their daring attacks
upon Plato and the Pentateuch, entirely
monopolized this branch of literary composition. In fact, the researches of Schleier-
macher, Ast, Socher, K. F. Hermann, Stein-
hart, Susemihl, and Ueberweg, concerning
the former, and those of Kuenen, Well-
hausen, Reuss, Schultz, Kautzsch, Stade,
and König in regard to the latter, had led
to the impression that Higher Criticism
was so indigenous to Germany that it could
not flourish in any other soil. It is with
feelings of just pride that I certify, in this
place, that not only is this not so, but that
that species of Higher Criticism which is
peculiarly American is equally exact, schol-
arly, and penetrating as the Teutonic, and
infinitely more novel and daring in its aim
and scope. Germany had been content
with impeaching the authenticity of the
Pentateuch, and revising the Alexandrine

Canon—subjects of equal antiquity with
the Pyramids—whereas, it was reserved
for an American to successfully question
the imputed authorship of plays which had
been in existence considerably less than
three centuries.   In the former case, it is
possible for the critic to bewilder the reader
by a showy exhibition of that ponderous
scholarship which the examination of the
works of antiquity requires.   In the latter,
attention cannot be cleverly diverted from
the only point at issue by learned digres-
sions on the proper use of the digamma,
or the relation of vowel-points to authorship.   The difference must strike every
intelligent observer as being exactly anal-
ogous to that which exists between those
prestidigitateurs who, separated from their
audience by the intervention of an orches-
tra and footlights, require all the accesso-
ries of stage machinery for the performance

of their tricks, and those clever jugglers who swallow needles and knives in the open air, and in the very centre of a gaping and admiring crowd. As the palm in legerdemain must assuredly be given to the latter, so, by parity of reasoning, superiority in the use of the Higher Criticism must be allowed to Mr. Ignatius Donnelly.

I am conscious of the necessity for curbing my pardonable enthusiasm so as not to exaggerate the praise which is the legitimate guerdon of that gentleman. I am perfectly willing to admit that Poe's clever story of the Gold Bug, and the investigations of the Potter Committee may have suggested to him the skilful use which may be made of cryptographs and ciphers, so that perhaps his *modus operandi* was not strictly original. But what I desire to emphasize is the daring and novel application which he has made of the principles of the

Higher Criticism. There would have been no novelty in his method had he selected as a subject the Homeric Myth, the Epistles of Phaleris, or Pentateuchal legislation. Such subjects have been discussed so frequently by prime ministers, diplomats, and divines as to be practically exhausted. But to prove by the Higher Criticism that that man was a forger who is the most revered of all English authors, whose statue adorns Central Park, whose plays are annually performed in many of our larger cities, whose birthplace was the only fixture in the whole United Kingdom, which, with the exception of Jumbo, Americans ever desired to import—such daring, novel, unprecedented use of the Higher Criticism proves conclusively to me, at least, that the present era of American literature, in spite of the conspicuous absence of pessimistic novelists and poets with a cult, is destined to occupy a brilliant position in the literary history of the world.

I have considered it superfluous to even indicate the substance of Mr. Donnelly's Higher Criticism. To future generations it will be a twice-told tale. I have, however, deemed it prudent, for the reputation of my age, to thus strongly emphasize the date of its original authorship. Time brings many jealousies in her train, and the future very grudgingly yields the credit of valuable discoveries to the past. As this application of the Higher Criticism to modern authorship inaugurated by Mr. Donnelly will be widely imitated, it is wise to thus definitely show that its origin must be sought in the Age of Cleveland. For I am quite convinced that it will be proven, at no distant time, that the Duke of Weimar was the real author of " Faust," and that Sir William Temple composed the " Tale of

a Tub." Nay, I will venture to predict,
that scarce half a century can elapse before it is demonstrated that Inspector Will-
iams, and not Inspector Byrnes, was the
collaborateur with Mr. Julian Hawthorn of
"An American Penman," and "A Tragic
Mystery," and that these works, ignorantly
viewed by contemporary society as having
been written with no higher purpose than
to amuse, were intended, as a matter of
fact, to be a valuable contribution to the
literature of municipal politics by containing in cipher the only complete and au-
thentic account in existence of the secret
history of removals and promotions in the
Police Board.

Two considerations, quite apart from
the proverbial dryness of legal topics, have
influenced me to avoid any detailed discussion of the condition of the law during

the present age. In the first place, it is
naturally impossible for a layman to com-
press such a vast body of statutes and
precedents within anything like a reasonable compass, nor have I been able to find
a single member of the bar who would accept a retainer to do the same, and give
me a written guarantee that the result of
his labors would be intelligible to anybody
except a judge of thirty years' experience
on the bench. But that which has chiefly
deterred me is the consideration that, even
if I did attempt some faulty and awkward di-
gest of our present laws, or employed some
attorney to do it for me, the task would be
toil wholly wasted. For I am quite convinced that if this book is read by posterity,
codification shall by that time have wholly
supplanted the present use of the Common
Law. By this means, the tangled maze of
customs, statutes, and precedents whereby

contracts, torts, and crimes are now defined, as well as the laws of procedure in
civil and criminal cases, will be made quite
intelligible to every layman of average intelligence—something to which the most
experienced lawyer in the land would not
now pretend.   I am, moreover, pretty well
convinced that that unfailing good-nature
of our legislators, which keeps them from
passing any bill of a very positive character, for fear of giving offence to some constituent, may be relied upon to transmit to
posterity the entire body of our present
laws, without any material alteration.   One
incidental result of codification will, therefore, be to present, in a systematic and
lucid fashion, and with sufficient exactitude
for the purposes of the antiquarian of the
future, what exists in the present age in an
obscure and chaotic state.

But there is a certain class of *obiter*

dicta which will not, in all likelihood, find a place in the codes of the future. Although not rising to the dignity of precedents, a familiarity with them is necessary, in order to intelligently comprehend many phases of contemporaneous legislation, and it is for this reason that I propose to record them at the close of the present chapter.

In the first place, I wish to give an exact definition of the term, "The City and County of New York." This grandiloquent phrase may possibly mislead posterity into conceiving of a municipality autonomous to the extent of having exclusive authority in all matters of a purely local nature. Such a conception would not only tend to much confusion in many instances, but do a positive injury to many innocent citizens by holding them responsible for matters over which they had absolutely no control. It is therefore eminently proper to state, that the territory and municipality of the City and County of New York are separated from each other by a considerable distance. The former is situated on Manhattan Island; the latter is located in an entirely different place. In this particular instance, there is a marked difference between the foreign and domestic policy of both the Republican and Democratic parties. Both unite in advocating Home Rule for Ireland, and both insist, with equal firmness, that New York shall be governed from Albany. Posterity must not infer from the above that there is not even the semblance of a regular city government. At stated intervals elections are held for a Mayor, Board of Aldermen, and other public officials, who succeed in investing themselves with sufficient bureaucratic functions to give at times the impression

that they constitute an actual, and not simply a nominal, municipality. Nor are these
city offices, though in a measure unnec-
essary, wholly destitute of importance.
Whenever any of them are abolished by
the municipality at Albany, the state and
national campaign fund incurs a corresponding decrease, the very existence of
which would be seriously jeopardized were
they abolished altogether ; while the memory of St. Patrick would suffer a considerable loss of dignity, were there no Alder-
manic Chamber to regularly adjourn on
the seventeenth of March, out of respect
for the day.

I am sincerely anxious that the gratify-
ing reputation for opposition to official
jobbery and corruption recently secured to
my age by the conviction of the Broadway bribe-takers may survive the present
century at least. I therefore appreciate the

importance of exactly acquainting posterity
with what is now regarded as constituting
the crime of asking or receiving a bribe.
All mole-hills seem equally small when
viewed by the naked eye, but a percepti-
ble difference can be noted in their height
when submitted to a closer inspection
under the microscope. Just so, while many
gratuities may seem equally corrupt to the
unaided eye of morality, a difference between *à priori* and *ex post facto* bribery
can be easily detected through the lens of
the law. Moreover, not only is there such
a difference, but different names are ap-
plied to each. The former is called a
felony, the latter a perquisite. I feel the
fullest assurance that posterity, if the foregoing distinction is only kept constantly in
view, will find no difficulty in lauding the
present age as the stern and unrelenting
foe of official bribe-taking.

I cannot close this chapter more appro-
priately than with a partial explanation of
the anomalous position occupied by corporations in the present age. The explanation can be only partial, because I
can urge no sufficient reason why corporations are allowed such enormous privileges.
They were originally granted, I believe,
on the theory that the recipients were a
benefit to the public, and therefore deserv-
ing of encouragement. But the actual
hostility of corporations to the common
weal has become so notorious that even
the inexhaustible resources of the law have
been insufficient to preserve that fiction
any longer. I must therefore frankly admit my inability to explain this aspect of
the subject. I am, however, more fortunate in being able to offer an explanation
of the narrow limit fixed to the liabilities
of corporations. They were long since

decided to have no souls, and are, therefore, unable to distinguish any more than
a cat or a dog between right and wrong.
It would, consequently, be absurd to im-
pose upon them anything like moral responsibility. It, moreover, I must confess,
seems illogical in the extreme that, in view
of the recent discoveries of science, which
have been noted in a previous chapter, the
same license which is allowed to corporations has not been extended to natural as
well as artificial persons. It is to be hoped
that the biological conception of the universe may speedily receive judicial notice,
whereby both these classes may obtain the
benefit of that limited liability, which is at
present monopolized by one of them. For
men, women, and even children are now
held to a strict account for erecting and
maintaining nuisances; the commission of
grand or petit larceny; and such acts of

criminal carelessness as result in injury to
the life, limb, or property of another,—all
of which is a monstrous injustice, when
science has conclusively demonstrated that
they also, like corporations, have no souls.